Try Not to Laugh Challenge!

Rules:

Pick your team, or go one on one.

Sit across from each other & make eye contact.

Take turns reading jokes to each other.

You can make silly faces, funny sound effects, etc.

When your opponent laughs, you get a point!

First team to win 3 points, Wins!

Telling Jokes Builds Confident Kids, & Laughter Makes Everyone Happy!

What Easter Bunny lives under the sea?

The Easter Mer-bunny!

What kind of bunny can't hop?

Dust bunnies!

Why didn't the anteater want to help the Easter Bunny?

It's Aard-vark!

Why can't the Easter Bunny travel to outer space?

Someone has to planet!

Who took the Easter Bunny's soap?

The robber duckie!

Who is in charge of sending messages for the Easter Bunny?

Tweeter cottontail!

Why did the Easter Bunny want the pasta to help him carry the Easter baskets?

He was stroganoff!

What is a sheep's favorite computer site?

Ewe-tube!

Who drives the Easter train?

A con-duck-tor!

Where do the Easter chicks live in London?

Cluckingham Palace!

What Easter Story do pugs like?

The Pugly Duckling!

Why shouldn't the Easter Bunny DAB backwards?

That would be BAD!

Who is a chick's favorite princess?

Peeping Beauty!

What do you call a cheerful egg?

Sunny-side up!

What do you call bunnies at summer camp?

Hoppy campers!

What happens when the Easter Bunny farts?

He tries to clear the hare!

What is a rooster's favorite song?

Let it Crow!

How does the Easter Bunny get by in computer class?

Bit by bit!

Who is the Easter Bunny's coolest friend?

The Hip-po!

What did the sleepy flower say to the bee?

Buzz off!

Who brings Easter eggs to little unicorns?

The Easter Bunni-corn!

Why didn't the Easter Bunny want the robot to help him?

He couldn't rust him!

What princess likes the Easter Bunny?

Ra-bun-zel!

What do hot cross buns say at Easter?

Happy Yeaster!

Why is it hard to get information from a duck?

He is a hard nut to quack!

Why does the Easter Bunny think the ducks are funny?

Because they like to quack jokes!

Where do you go to see Easter art?

Art eggs-hibit!

What do you get when you cross a pig and a spider?

Bacon and legs!

Why did the Easter Bunny decide not to waste time looking for something on the internet?

He didn't feel like going down a rabbit hole!

Why were the kids excited?

It's Easter for peeps sake!

What do ducks eat for lunch?

Soup & quackers!

What do you get when you cross a bunny & a frog?

A bunny ribbit!

Why are flowers so popular?

They have lots of buds!

Why was the Easter egg worried about his cracked shell?

Because he couldn't egg-nore it any longer!

What do little bunnies like to eat for lunch?

Hoppy meals!

How does the Easter Bunny hide all those eggs?

He plays it by ear!

What board game does the Easter Bunny like to play?

Mon-hop-oly!

Why do little chicks go to the doctor?

For their rooster shots!

What did the Easter Bunny say to the singing mermaid?

Your song is out of tuna!

What dinosaur helps the Easter Bunny hide eggs?

Tricera-hops!

Did you hear about the peacock that crossed the road?

It was a colorful tale!

Did you hear that the Easter lily finally bloomed for Easter?

Last bud not least!

Where does the Easter duck live in England?

Duckingham Palace!

What do you call a bunny who gossips?

Busy-bunny!

How does the avocado help the Easter Bunny exercise?

Avocardio!

What is the Easter Bunny afraid of?

Spring Fever!

What happened when the bees dropped their honey?

It was a sticky situation!

Why do the Easter eggs hang out with Humpty Dumpty?

They are willing to whisk it!

What do you call a grumpy bee?

A grumble bee!

Why doesn't the Easter Bunny buy yogurt?

It was all Greek to him!

What is another name for a bunch of bees?

A pretty good report card!

What does the Easter Bunny do at the mall?

Shop until you hop!

How does the Easter Bunny know where to hide the all of the eggs?

He has lots of eggs-perience!

What did the Easter Bunny ask the sick flower?

Are you feeling bouquet?

Who do you call to find missing Easter eggs?

Sherlock Hops!

Who brings Easter eggs to all the little mermaids?

The Easter Peep-maid!

What is a frog's favorite video game?

Wart-nite!

Where does the Easter Bunny live?

No bunny knows!

What do you say to the Easter Bunny when he leaves for vacation?

Hoppy trails!

Why do seedlings make good cheerleaders?

They are always rooting for you!

Who are the Easter superheros?

Peepman & Robin!

What kind of game do bunnies like to play?

Hare hockey!

What kind of garden does a pastry chef have?

A flour garden!

Do you know that Easter lilies like to play tricks?

Yup, they like pollen your leg!

Who has more lives than a cat?

A frog, he croaks every night!

What kind of candy do little bunnies like?

Lolli-hops!

Who takes forever to find his Easter eggs?

The sloth!

How did the chick get to the Easter party on time?

She used her alarm cluck!

Where do Easter eggs work?

The oval office!

How does the Easter Bunny eat his chinese noodles?

With hop-sticks!

Why is the turtle lots of fun to be with?

He came out of his shell!

Where do you find ducks in the morning?

At the quack of dawn!

Why are Easter eggs good at playing "Try Not to Laugh Challenge" game?

They know not to crack a smile!

Did you hear that the Easter Bunny fell in love?

Love was in the hare!

Rhyme Time!

Did you hear about the duck that won the lottery?

A lucky ducky!

What kind of rabbits tell jokes?

A funny bunny!

What do you call a bunny with a sweet tooth?

Honey bunny!

What happens when you run into an Easter bee?

Spring sting!

Why do we decorate eggs?

It's a spring thing!

What do ducks like to eat?

Quack snack!

Why don't chicks drink soda?

A chirp burp!

What kind of Easter candy does a princess eat?

Queen beans!

What do you call a frog joke?

A croak joke!

What is the funniest Easter flower?

Silly Lily!

What do you call a frog that takes all the lily pads for himself?

A frog hog!

What do you call the Easter Bunny?

A rare hare!

Where do Easter rainbows come from?

Easter Unicorn farts!

What three words does the chicken's Constitution start with?

We the Peeps!

What letter should you stay away from?

Bee!

Why were the peeps forbidden to send emails?

They were using fowl language!

Who is the slowest Easter Bunny?

The Sloth-ster Bunny!

Where does the Easter Bunny stay on vacation?

In a hare-bnb!

What kind of Easter candy do mermaids eat?

Shelly beans!

Did you know the Easter Bunny eats pasta every day?

It is his daily rotini!

Why did the Easter Bunny think he may have too many jelly beans this year?

His house was jam-packed!

The Easter Kitty is hiding the Easter eggs this year!

Just kitten!

How do all the Spring animals send messages?

Critter twitter!

Why wasn't the pan laughing at the broken egg?

Because the yolk was on him!

How do dogs like their eggs?

Pooched!

What is an Easter egg's favorite snack?

Shello!

What do you call an avocado in church?

Holy Guacamole!

What do you call robins that are sunbathing?

Baskin' Robins!

What do you call a lamb covered in chocolate?

A chocolate baa!

What kind of Easter candy do ogres eat?

Smelly beans!

How do fairy tales with bunnies end?

Hoppily ever after!

What chicken sucks the juice out of the Easter Bunny's vegetables?

Peep-ula!

How does the Easter Bunny get into bed?

With a hop, skip & a jump!

What kind of music does an avocado like?

Guac & Roll!

Why are eggs afraid of pastry chefs?

Can't make a cake without breaking some eggs!

Which way did the Easter computer go?

It went data way!

What did the cell phone say to the Easter Bunny?

Have your selfie a Hoppy Easter!

How do bunnies share computer files?

Hare drop!

I heard the Easter Bunny swallowed a dollar.

There is no change yet!

What insect is afraid of getting wet?

A firefly!

Should you let a garden gnome take care of your garden for you?

Of course, that's a gnome brainer!

What kind of cactus likes to greet Easter?

Aloe Easter!

The Easter Bunny doesn't like it when someone puts him on the spot.

Don't you?

What show about cute bears does the Easter Bunny watch?

Hare Bears!

Why can you always tell what Jack & Jill are going to do?

They are so easy to read!

Knock, knock.

Who's there?

Spring.

Spring who?

Spring to it & open this door!

Knock, knock.

Who's there?

Bunny.

Bunny who?

Some bunny open this door!

Knock, knock.

Who's there?

Peeps.

Peeps who?

Power to the Peeps!

Knock, knock.

Who's there?

Oink.

Oink who?

Oink you glad it's Easter!

What do rabbit musicians play?

Hare guitars!

Where does the Easter Bunny go after second grade?

Fur-ed grade!

What did the avocado say to the fork?

You gauc my world!

What kind of vegetable does Santa grow?

Chilly peppers!

What kind of peppers do ghouls grow?

Ghost peppers!

Why did the garden fairy want a round table?

So no one could corner her!

What do you call an Easter Bunny in space?

An Easter-naut!

Why did the Easter egg plan a party?

She wanted to shell-ebrate!

What did the Easter Bunny say when he walked into the room?

Hare I am!

Why does the foal chew with his mouth open?

He has bad stable manners!

What do you get when you cross an Easter bee with a eagle?

An Easter Beagle!

What do you call a clueless Easter egg?

Egg-noramus!

Why couldn't the mermaid go on the egg hunt?

She was feeling a little under the water!

What insect speaks in a confused way?

A bumble-bee!

What do you call a clumsy bee?

A stumble bee!

What do dachshunds sing at Easter?

Here comes wiener cottontail, hopping down the bunny trail..!

How do you make an egg roll?

You push it!

What do you call a chicken in a shell costume?

An egg!

What kind of musical instrument does a pig play?

A key-boar-d!

What are Easter eggs afraid of?

Eggbeaters!

What dinosaur likes Easter egg hunts?

A St-egg-osaurus!

Did you hear about the chicken who only lays eggs in the winter?

She's no spring chicken!

Did you hear about the funny chicken?

He was a peeps of work!

Why was the Easter egg worried about going out in public?

Because he was showing a little crack!

What is a leprechaun's favorite kind of test?

Fill in the bank!
(Fill in the blank)

What do the Easter Bunny farts smell like?

Chocolate!

How does President Bunny travel?

In Hare force one!

Can llamas find the Easter eggs?

No prob-llama!

What do baby morning doves say?

Coo coo!

What word game do Easter eggs play?

Scramble!

What do little bunnies sing in preschool?

You are my Bun-shine!

Knock, knock.

Who's there?

Cottontail.

Cottontail who?

Cottontail you where the Easter Bunny lives!

Knock, knock.

Who's there?

Peeps.

Peeps who?

Imagine World Peeps!

How did the mermaid pay for her Easter candy?

With a credit cod!

Why doesn't T. Rex like egg hunts?

His arms are too short for picking up eggs!

What kind of rabbit collects insects?

Bugs Bunny!

What do eggs need special sunglasses for?

A solar egg-clipse!

Why was the Easter Bunny going to the hairdresser?

He was having a bad Hare day!

Why do frogs like April Fools?

They are practical croakers!

Where does the Easter Bunny go to find out the weather for Easter?

Frog-casters!

Why do Easter eggs like April Fools Day?

They like practical yolks!

Why did the boy want a GPS?

So he could find his Easter eggs!

Where does the little squirrel go before kindergarten?

Tree school!

Why was the chocolate bunny a basket case?

He was hollow inside!

How can April jump high?

Spring!

Why did the chick write the book report?

To get eggs-tra credit!

Knock, knock.

Who's there?

Howard.

Howard who?

Howard you like a chocolate bunny?

Knock, knock.

Who's there?

Andrew.

Andrew who?

Andrew a flower on my egg!

What kind of hamburger does the Easter Bunny like?

The W-hop-per!

What is the Spring version of the Blue's Clues TV show?

Ewe's Clues!

What season is it when you are on a pogo stick?

Spring time!

What would bears be without bees?

Ears!

How did the tree feel when Spring started?

Re-leaved!

What did the Easter Bunny say when he finished hiding the Easter eggs?

I'm outta hare!

Who helps the Easter Bunny deliver baskets under the sea?

The Easter Purr-maid!

Who keeps the Easter Bunny's carrots safe?

The gnomes are garden them!

Why is the Mom Peep good at breaking up chicken fights?

She knows how to keep the peeps!

Who is the sloth's favorite princess?

Slow White!

How do you know if the Easter Bunny is mad?

You can see it in his bunny language! (body language)

What is a poop emoji's favorite holiday?

April Stools Day!

What kind of beans don't make you fart?

Jelly beans!

What kind of flower melts?

A butter-cup!

Who writes plays for birds?

Shakes-sparrow!

Why didn't the Easter Bunny answer the door?

Because no-bunny was home!

What did the ladybug say after lunch?

That hit the spot!

Why did the earthworm buy his house?

Because he got it dirt cheap!

Why was it naptime for the little bunnies?

Mom bunny needed them out of her hare!

How does the Easter Bunny hide all those eggs?

He hops to it!

What did the baby lamb say when she found a rotten egg?

Ewwe!

What do you call a modest bee?

A humble bee!

Why did the Easter Bunny want to go to the moon?

He wanted to be a space eggs-plorer!

What do bunnies eat when they watch movies?

Hop-corn!

Are peeps good at egg hunts?

Yup, finding eggs is a peeps of cake!

What did the Easter egg say to the dinosaur?

You are eggs-tinct!

What is a kitten's favorite color?

Purr-ple!

The Easter Bunny is an expert at filling Easter Baskets.

He really knows his stuff!

Why did the boy bring his comb to the egg hunt?

He wanted to comb the yard for eggs!

Why did the little chick put lipstick on her forehead?

She was trying to make-up her mind!

Why did the family looked stressed out at Easter dinner?

They had a lot on their plates!

What do kids like on their cupcakes at Easter?

Eggs-tra rainbow sprinkles!

Why was the boy in trouble for eating his sister's chocolate eggs?

He didn't have a good eggs-cuse!

How does the Easter Bunny deliver Easter baskets to the birds?

In a hot Hare balloon!

Why do the chicks want to work on the hot Hare balloon?

Every day they get a raise!

Why didn't the Easter chicks laugh at the rainbow joke?

It was over their head!

Where do rabbits ski?

On the bunny slope!

What do spelling bees like about kindergarten?

Show & Spell!
(Show & Tell)

Who won't share the hedge in the garden?

The hedge-hog!

How do the chicks know they are in trouble?

When the Easter Bunny gives them the Hare-y eyeball!

How did the Easter Bunny feel about the peeps?

They will be friends fur-ever!

What insect melts on a warm spring day?

A butter-fly!

What did Snow White call her chicken?

Egg white!

What is a sloth's favorite exercise?

Yoga!

Where do leprechauns fart?

At the end of the rainbow!

What did the giant Easter daffodil say?

I'm kind of a big dil!

What grows on yolk trees?

Egg corns!

What does every kitty have?

Purr-ents!

What does T. Rex think about Easter?

Easter is Rex-cellent!

What duck sucks the juice out of the Easter Bunny's vegetables?

Duck-ula!

Knock, knock.

Who's there?

Peeping.

Peeping who?

Just peeping around to see if I can find my Easter basket!

Knock, knock.

Who's there?

Woolly.

Woolly who?

I woolly can't wait to look for my Easter Basket!

Knock, knock.

Who's there?

Wanda.

Wanda who?

I Wanda eat my jelly beans!

Knock, knock.

Who's there?

Eggs.

Eggs who?

Eggs-actly how many eggs do we have to find?

Knock, knock.

Who's there?

Lettuce.

Lettuce who?

Lettuce help decorate the eggs!

Knock, knock.

Who's there?

Donut.

Donut who?

Donut worry, the Easter will come!

Knock, knock.

Who's there?

Bunny.

Bunny who?

Some bunny is eating my Easter candy!

Knock, knock.

Who's there?

Ears.

Ears who?

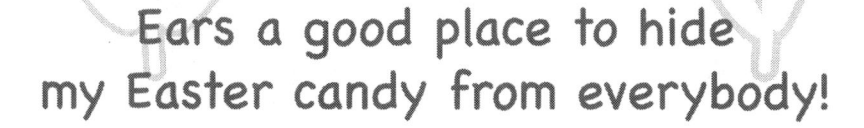

Ears a good place to hide
my Easter candy from everybody!

Knock, knock.

Who's there?

Abby.

Abby who?

Abby Easter!

Knock, knock.

Who's there?

Usher.

Usher who?

Usher hope this is the last Knock-knock joke!

Why are there so many chicks at Easter time?

They are very peep-ular!

What do you call an Easter pokemon?

Peep-achu!

What game do baby chicks play?

Peep-a-boo!

What is a hornet's favorite movie?

Beauty & the Bee-ast!

What is a egg's favorite song?

The Farmer in the Shell!

What kind of bee cuts down trees?

Bee-ver!

What is a chick's favorite game?

Hide & peep!

Why can't a snail win an argument?

It doesn't have a leg to stand on!

How do we know the snail ate the Easter candy?

He was seen at the scene of the slime!

What do you call someone who draws flowers?

A budding artist!

What did the gnome say when he got home?

There's no place like gnome!

What did the Easter Bunny say after hiding all the eggs?

That's all, yolks!

Also Available from Howling Moon Books

Also Available from Howling Moon Books

Also Available from Howling Moon Books